FOREX SWING TRADING FOR BEGINNERS

Mastering the Art of Swing Trading in Forex

James Willy

Copyright © 2024 James Willy

All rights reserved. No part of this book may be reproduced, distributed, or transmitted in any form or by any means, including photocopying, recording, or other electronic or mechanical methods, without the prior written permission of the author, except in the case of brief quotations embodied in critical reviews and certain other noncommercial uses permitted by copyright law.

CONTENT

INTRODUCTION — 7

The Exciting World of Forex Swing Trading — 7

CHAPTER 1 — 15

Understanding Forex and Swing Trading — 15

    The Forex Market: A Trader's Goldmine — 15

    Swing Trading: Riding Market Waves — 17

    Why Forex Swing Trading Could Be Your Game Changer — 19

    Personal Experience: A Turning Point — 21

CHAPTER 2 — 24

Building Your Forex Foundation — 24

    Currency pairs: The lifeblood of Forex — 24

        Major Pairs: — 25

        Minor Pairs: — 25

        Exotic Pairs — 25

    Decoding Forex Quotes and Charts — 26

    Leverage: A Double-Edged Sword — 28

CHAPTER 3 — 31

The Swing Trader's Arsenal — 31

Technical Analysis: Your Market Roadmap	32
The key components of technical analysis	32
Chart Patterns	32
Head and Shoulders	32
Double Tops and Bottoms	32
Triangles	33
Trend Lines	33
Support and Resistance	33
Indicators	33
Fundamental Analysis: Understanding Market Movers	34
Blending Technical and Fundamentals for Best Results	37

CHAPTER 4   41

Crafting Your Swing Trading Strategy	**41**
Entry and Exit Strategies that Work	41
Trend-following entries	42
Breakout Entries	42
Reverse Entries:	43
Exit plans are equally important	43
Set Stop-Loss and Take-Profit: Your Safety Net	44
Position Sizing: Balancing Risk and Rewards	45
Percentage-Based Sizing	45
Fixed Dollar Amount	46
Use Volatility-Based Sizing:	46
Adapting To Market Conditions	46

CHAPTER 5 — 51

Risk Management: Protecting Your Capital — 51
    The 1% Rule is a lifesaver for beginners — 51
    Emotional Control: Understanding the Trader's Mindset — 53
        Stick to Your Plan — 53
        Use Stop-Losses — 53
        Practice Mindfulness — 54
        Keep a trading journal — 54
        Avoid overtrading — 54
    Dealing with Losses: Converting Setbacks into Comebacks — 55
    The risk-reward ratio is the key to long-term profitability — 56
    Diversification of Forex Trading — 58
    Continuous Risk Assessment — 59

CHAPTER 6 — 62

Put It All Together: Your Trading Plan — 62
    Setting realistic goals and expectations — 62
    Creating a Personalized Trading Schedule — 64
    Define Your Trading Strategy. — 65
    Back-testing and Forward Testing: Your Strategy — 66
    Adapting Your Plan As You Grow — 67
    Key elements of a comprehensive trading plan — 69

CHAPTER 7 — 72

Real-Life Swing Trading Case Studies — 72

Case Study 1: Riding the Trend in EUR/USD	72
Case Study 2: How to Navigate a Range-Bound Market in GBP/JPY	74
Case Study 3: Managing a Losing Trade in AUD/USD	76
Lessons from Case Studies	78

CHAPTER 8 — 82

Evolving as a Forex Swing Trader — 82

- Continuous Learning and Improvement. — 82
- Staying ahead of market trends — 85
  - Embrace Technology: — 85
- Developing a Sustainable Trading Career — 87
  - Risk Management Evolution — 87
  - Diversification Strategies — 88
  - Develop a Business Mindset — 88
  - Continuous approach Refinement — 89

CONCLUSION — 92

Your Journey Begins — 92

- Recap: Key Swing Trading Principles — 92
- Encouragement and Final Thoughts — 95

Introduction

The Exciting World of Forex Swing Trading

In the broad ocean of financial markets, forex trading shines as a light of opportunity, attracting traders from all walks of life with its siren call of possible rewards. However, for many, this enticing region is cloaked in mystery, with its depths appearing impenetrable. Enter forex swing trading, a method that strikes the ideal balance between the frenzied pace of day trading and the slow fluctuations of long-term investing.

As you read through the pages of "Forex Swing Trading For Beginners: Mastering the Art of Swing Trading in Forex," imagine yourself as a surfer on the edge of a wave.

The forex market is like an ocean, always changing, sometimes peaceful, sometimes stormy. Swing trading is your surfboard, allowing you to ride these waves with skill while profiting as currencies fluctuate.

But why Forex? Why not stocks, commodities, or other financial assets? The explanation lies in the currency market's sheer size and accessibility. This worldwide marketplace operates 24 hours a day, five days a week, with a daily trade volume that eclipses all other financial markets combined. It's a place where central banks, multinational corporations, and ordinary traders like you and me come together, each playing a role in the big dance of currency valuation.

Swing trading in an active market provides a distinct advantage.

Swing traders, as opposed to day traders, who must continually monitor their screens, and position traders, who may hold trades for months, operate in a sweet spot. They seek to capture medium-term trends by holding positions for days or weeks. This strategy provides for a more balanced lifestyle while still providing the opportunity for big earnings.

As we progress through this book, we'll explore the complexities of forex swing trading, beginning with the fundamentals. You will learn how to understand currency pairings, which are mysterious symbols such as EUR/USD or GBP/JPY that constitute the foundation of forex trading. We'll look at how these pairs change in relation to one another, driven by a complicated web of economic, political, and social influences.

But knowledge isn't enough. To properly master forex swing trading, you need a solid toolkit. Technical and fundamental analysis are useful tools in this context. Technical analysis, with its plethora of charts, indicators, and patterns, will serve as your crystal ball, allowing you to forecast future price moves based on past data. Meanwhile, fundamental analysis can help you understand the real-world events that influence currency valuations, such as interest rate choices and geopolitical concerns.

As your guide on this adventure, I'll share insights gained from years of experience navigating these waters. You'll learn how to develop a swing trading strategy that fits your objectives and risk tolerance. We'll look at how to place stop-loss and take-profit orders, those critical lines in the sand that safeguard your capital and lock in your earnings. You'll learn the value of position sizing, a skill that can make the difference between long-term profits and account-draining losses.

But maybe the most important lesson - one that took me years to fully understand - is the need of risk management.

In the realm of forex trading, capital preservation is essential. The excitement of a large triumph can be swiftly replaced by the misery of a blown account.

That is why we will spend substantial time building a strong risk management approach, including the golden 1% rule, which has rescued numerous trading accounts from catastrophe.

Throughout this book, you will uncover real-life case studies - both successes and failures from my own trading career. These stories serve not just as demonstrations of fundamental principles, but also as reminders that every trader, regardless of experience, is constantly learning. We'll deconstruct these transactions to understand the reasoning behind each decision, the lessons learnt, and how to apply these insights to your own trading.

As we approach the end of our trip together, we'll look ahead to see how you might grow as a forex swing trader.

The marketplaces are constantly changing, so you must adapt and expand. We'll talk about how to keep on top of market trends, learn continuously, and develop a long-term trading profession.

Let me relate a personal tale to demonstrate the transformational potential of forex swing trading. Several years ago, I was working a 9-to-5 job and felt caught in the rat race. I came into forex trading and struggled at first, as do many newbies. I was overtrading, taking on too much risk, and allowing my emotions guide my actions. But then I discovered swing trading, which was like finding the missing piece of the puzzle.

I have clear memories of my first successful swing trade. It was a EUR/USD trade held for a little more than a week. I painstakingly examined the charts, factored in impending economic announcements, and established obvious entry and exit points.

As the trade went exactly as planned, I felt a surge of excitement, not just from the winnings, but also from the realization that I had finally solved the code.

That transaction was a turning moment in my journey. Over the next few months and years, I adjusted my strategy, weathered both winning and losing streaks, and gradually established a track record of steady profitability. Today, forex swing trading has given me not just financial freedom but also a sense of purpose that I never had in my former job.

As you read this book, keep in mind that your experience with FX swing trading is unique to you. The ideas and tactics we'll discuss will serve as your compass and map, but the course you choose will be unique to you. Embrace the learning process, maintain discipline, and, most importantly, never stop evolving.

Welcome to the world of Forex swing trading. Your quest to mastery starts now.

CHAPTER 1

Understanding Forex and Swing Trading

For newbies, the world of forex trading might appear to be a maze, with twists and turns that confuse even the most dedicated hopefuls. However, amid this convoluted maze lies a strategy that has enormous potential: swing trading. Let us go on a trip to demystify forex and swing trading, revealing the opportunities that await.

The Forex Market: A Trader's Goldmine

Consider a market that never sleeps, where trillions of dollars are exchanged everyday, and where you can profit from both increasing and decreasing prices.

Welcome to the Forex Market, the world's largest and most liquid financial market.

Forex, or foreign exchange, is a global marketplace for trading national currencies. Unlike stock markets, which have regular hours, forex trading occurs around the clock, five days a week. This 24-hour nature originates from the market's global reach, with major financial centres in London, New York, Tokyo, and Sydney functioning in separate time zones.

The FX market is enormous in size. On an average day, more than $6.6 trillion in currencies are traded. Because of this high liquidity, you can buy and sell currencies instantaneously under typical market conditions, without having to worry about large price swings caused by single trade.

But what fuels this vast market? At its essence, forex trading is swapping one currency for another. Governments, banks, corporations, and investors all participate in this market for a variety of reasons, including enabling international trade and gambling on economic trends.

For independent traders like us, the forex market provides distinct advantages:

1. **Accessibility:** Online trading platforms allow you to start trading forex with minimal funds.

2. **Leverage:** Forex brokers provide leverage, enabling traders to control greater positions with less money. (But beware, leverage is a two-edged sword!)

3. **Flexibility:** Profit from rising and declining markets by buying or selling currency pairings.

4. **Diversity:** There are numerous currency pairs to pick from, ensuring there is always an opportunity in the market.

Swing Trading: Riding Market Waves

Now that we've set the scenario for the forex market, let's focus on our preferred strategy: swing trading. If day trading is like sprinting and long-term investment is like running a marathon, swing trading is the trading world's middle-distance race.

Swing trading seeks to collect profit in a currency pair spanning a few days to many weeks. As a swing trader, you want to profit from the "swings" in currency values, which are the medium-term ups and downs that occur as part of bigger trends or ranges.

The beauty of swing trading is found in its equilibrium. Unlike day traders, who must be glued to their screens all day, swing traders can analyse the markets, place trades, and then take a break, enabling their positions to develop over time. This makes swing trading a good strategy for people who cannot (or do not want to) devote all of their time to trading.

Swing trading has several key qualities, including:

1. Time Frame: Trades usually last a few days to weeks.

2. Analysis: Integrates technical and fundamental analysis to provide a comprehensive view of the market.

3. Risk Management: Better risk control than long-term trading.

4. Frequency: Not as regular as day trading, but more active than position trading.

Why Forex Swing Trading Could Be Your Game Changer.

So, why should you consider forex swing trading? Let us break it down:

1. Swing trading offers a balanced lifestyle as it does not demand constant market monitoring, allowing for a day job or other responsibilities.

2. Reduced stress: Compared to day trading, longer holding periods allow for less frequent decision-making.

3. Cost-effective: With fewer trades, transaction costs are lower than day trading.

4. Swing trading captures more of a trend than day trading.

5. Longer durations allow for full trading analysis and planning.

6. Suitable for volatile markets: Swing trading capitalises on price swings in forex markets.

However, it is critical to recognise that forex swing trading is not a get-rich-quick plan. It demands commitment, discipline, and a desire to learn and adapt. You'll need to master technical and fundamental analysis, risk management, and trading psychology.

As we go through this book, we'll go further into each of these topics, giving you the knowledge and tools you need to become a competent forex swing trader.

Personal Experience: A Turning Point

Allow me to relate a personal experience that demonstrates the effectiveness of forex swing trading. Early in my trading career, I was drawn to the attraction of day trading. The rapid pace and prospect for quick profit appeared alluring. However, I quickly found myself burnt out, anxious, and, worst of all, routinely losing money.

During this low period, I discovered swing trading. I have clear memories of my first successful swing trade. The AUD/USD trade was based on a combination of technical signals and incoming economic data. I entered the trade on Monday, established my stop-loss and take-profit levels, and then waited.

The most difficult thing was fighting the impulse to constantly check my position. But as the days went, I noticed the trade shifting in my favour. By Friday, it had reached my take-profit level, resulting in a 3% increase in my account.

This trade was a revelation. I not only made a profit, but I did so without the stress and time commitment associated with day trading. It was the start of a new chapter in my trading journey.

As we begin this investigation of forex swing trading, keep in mind that every successful trader started where you are today. With effort, continual study, and the appropriate approach, you can also master the art of swing trading in the FX market.

Enhance Your Learning with Exclusive Video Access!

Thank you for choosing this book as your guide to mastering Forex trading. To help you get the most out of your learning experience, I have included a special video series that complements the concepts covered in this book.

These videos provide practical demonstrations, real-time chart analysis, and in-depth explanations to help you apply what you've learned. You'll find the access link at the end of the book, allowing you to dive deeper into the world of Forex trading.

Make sure to visit the link after you finish reading this book for a more interactive and hands-on approach to mastering Forex trading.

Let's move to the next chapter…

CHAPTER 2

Building Your Forex Foundation

As we delve deeper into the world of forex swing trading, it's critical to lay a strong foundation. Think of this chapter as the foundation for your trading adventure. We'll look at the fundamental building pieces that any forex trader, particularly swing traders, must grasp inside and out.

Currency pairs: The lifeblood of Forex

Currency pairs are fundamental to forex trading. These are the assets we trade, the vehicles that transport our profits (or losses). But, what exactly are they?

A currency pair is essentially a quote for two separate currencies, with the value of one being stated against the other. The first currency in the pair is referred to as the base currency, and the second as the quote currency.

For example, in the EUR/USD pair, EUR is the base currency and USD is the quotation currency. If the EUR/USD is trading at 1.2000, it signifies that one euro equals 1.2 US dollars.

Currency pairs are usually divided into three categories:

Major Pairs: These include the US dollar paired with major currencies such as the euro, Japanese yen, British pound, and Swiss franc. Examples are EUR/USD, USD/JPY, GBP/USD, and USD/CHF. These are the most liquid and actively traded pairs.

Minor Pairs: Also known as cross-currency pairs, these do not involve the USD. Examples are EUR/GBP, GBP/JPY, and EUR/CHF.

Exotic Pairs: A major currency is paired with a currency from a smaller or emerging economy, such as USD/SGD

(US dollar/Singapore dollar) or EUR/TRY (Euro/Turkish lira).

Swing traders are likely to focus on major and minor pairs. These provide the optimum balance of liquidity (easy of entering and quitting trades) and volatility (price movement that generates profits).

Decoding Forex Quotes and Charts.

Now that we know what currency pairings are, let's look at how they're quoted and depicted on charts.

Forex quotes always include two prices: the bid and ask prices. The bid is the price at which you can sell the base currency, and the ask is the price at which you can buy it. The spread is the difference between these prices, and it essentially represents the cost of trading.

For example, if the EUR/USD quote is 1.2000/1.2002, you can sell euros for 1.2000 and buy them at 1.2002 dollars. The spread here is two pips.

In terms of pips, this is another important idea. A pip, or "percentage in point," is often the smallest price change that a currency pair may make. For most pairs, a pip represents the fourth decimal point. So if EUR/USD moves from 1.2000 to 1.2001, it's a one-pip move.

Charts are graphic representations of price changes over time.

The three most popular types of charts in forex are:

1. Line charts visualise closing prices over time using a line.

2. Bar charts indicate opening, high, low, and closing prices for a given time period.

3. Candlestick charts provide a visual picture of price action, similar to bar charts.

These are particularly popular among swing traders due to their ability to vividly display price patterns.

As a swing trader, you'll probably spend a lot of time analyzing candlestick charts on the daily and 4-hour timeframe. These strike an excellent compromise between recording significant movements and filtering out short-term noise.

Leverage: A Double-Edged Sword.

One of the distinguishing characteristics of forex trading is the availability of leverage. Leverage helps you to manage a huge position with a small quantity of capital. For example, using 100:1 leverage, you can own a $100,000 position with only $1,000 in your account.

This may sound very appealing, and leverage can help you increase your revenues. However, and this is critical, it amplifies your losses. Many inexperienced traders have ruined their accounts by exploiting leverage.

Swing traders often utilise smaller leverage than day traders. This is because your positions will be open for longer periods of time, exposing you to a wider range of price movements. A general rule of thumb is to never risk more than 1-2% of your account value on a single trade, regardless of leverage.

In order to illustrate the significance of recognising the value of leverage, here is a personal story:

Early in my trading career, I was drawn to the attraction of high leverage. I had a tiny account and believed that employing 200:1 leverage was the fastest way to expand it. I took a huge EUR/USD trade, confident in my analysis.

At first, the trade went my way, and I was overjoyed. But then the market turned. Within hours, my account had lost half of its value. I was compelled to close the trade with a large loss.

This terrible incident taught me a vital lesson about the risks of excessive leverage. From that point forward, I took a more conservative approach, rarely utilizing more than 10:1 leverage for swing bets. This enabled me to withstand the inevitable lost trades without jeopardizing my entire account.

What's the key takeaway? Leverage is a tool, not a quick path to wealth. Use it prudently.

Bringing Everything Together

As we conclude this chapter, analyze how these fundamental parts work together in a typical swing trade.

Assume you are analyzing the GBP/USD pair. The daily chart shows a bullish pattern, which is reinforced by favorable UK economic statistics. You've decided to open a long position.

The current quotation is 1.3800/1.3802. You buy at the ask price of 1.3802 with 5:1 leverage. Your stop-loss is placed 50 pips lower at 1.3752, and your take-profit is 150 pips higher at 1.3952.

You study the trade over the next week, watching as the pound strengthens versus the dollar. Finally, after five days, your take-profit is reduced. You effectively captured a 150-pip move, proving the effectiveness of swing trading in forex.

This example demonstrates how understanding currency pairs, chart analysis, and judicious leverage may all contribute to a successful swing trade.

As we progress through this book, we'll expand on these fundamental notions, investigating more sophisticated strategies and techniques.

CHAPTER 3

The Swing Trader's Arsenal

In the volatile world of forex swing trading, knowledge truly is power. This chapter digs into the basic tools that are the foundation of any good swing trader's strategy.

We'll look at both technical and fundamental analysis, and how to combine both for the best outcomes.

Technical Analysis: Your Market Roadmap

Consider technical analysis to be your trusted GPS in the trading world. It is based on the idea that past price behaviour might predict future moves. Swing traders must understand technical analysis to determine entry and exit locations, as well as probable trend reversals.

The key components of technical analysis

Chart Patterns: Visual forms on price charts indicate anticipated market moves. Common patterns include the following:

Head and Shoulders: A reverse pattern that resembles a head and two shoulders.

Double Tops and Bottoms: The presence of double tops and bottoms signals the possibility of a trend reversal.

Triangles: These patterns indicate either a continuation or a reversal depending on the direction of the breakout. There is more to chart pattern

Trend Lines: These simple but effective tools connect highs and lows to determine market direction.

Support and Resistance: These levels serve as floor and ceiling for price changes. Identifying them might help you anticipate upcoming bounces or breakouts.

Indicators: Calculations based on price and volume might provide valuable data.

Smoothing price data with moving averages can reveal trends.

- The RSI: A tool for gauging market sentiment in times of excessive buying or selling.
- -Moving Average Convergence Divergence (MACD) identifies momentum and probable trend shifts.

I recall a particularly profitable GBP/JPY swing trade in which technical analysis played an important role. The daily chart revealed a clear uptrend, with the price continually following an ascending trendline. When price returned to this trendline, which coincided with a previous resistance level that had become support, I saw an opportunity. The RSI had also crossed into oversold area, indicating a possible bounce.

I opened a long position and set my stop loss below the trendline and support level. Over the next two weeks, the pair rebounded rapidly, reaching my take-profit level for a tidy 250-pip profit. This trade demonstrated how numerous technical indicators can combine to provide high-probability setups.

Fundamental Analysis: Understanding Market Movers.

Technical analysis informs us what the market is doing, and fundamental analysis explains why. It entails examining the economic, social, and political aspects that influence currency values.

The key elements of fundamental analysis are:

1. Economic indicators provide information about a country's economic health.

GDP is a broad indicator of economic activity.

- Employment reports, including non-farm payrolls in the US.

Inflation rates are often tracked by the Consumer Price Index (CPI).

Central bank choices on interest rates have a considerable impact on currency values.

2. Political events like elections, policy changes, and geopolitical conflicts can trigger significant currency swings.

3. Market Sentiment: Market sentiment can influence currency trends.

Understanding these elements is essential for swing traders. While we may not react to every news release, being aware of the big picture allows us to make more educated decisions.

I learnt the value of fundamental analysis the hard way. Early in my trading career, I held a sizable long position in USD/CAD based only on technical indicators. The chart appeared bullish, and I felt secure in my trade.

However, I had neglected an important piece of fundamental data: the imminent Bank of Canada interest rate announcement. The central bank unexpectedly boosted interest rates, prompting the Canadian dollar to rise substantially. My position suddenly shifted against me, resulting in a substantial loss.

This experience taught me to never overlook the fundamental terrain, even if the technical appear promising. It's a lesson I still remember today.

Blending Technical and Fundamentals for Best Results

The ultimate power of forex swing trading comes from combining technical and fundamental analysis. This holistic strategy offers a more complete picture of the market, boosting the likelihood of successful trades.

Here is how you could combine these approaches:

1. Use economic patterns and central bank policies to predict currency changes over time.

2. Use technical analysis to determine the best entry and exit positions after identifying a fundamental trend.

3. Confirm signals: When technical and fundamental indicators match, it indicates a promising trading opportunity.

4. Manage risk: Set stop-losses based on technical levels (e.g., support and resistance) and keep an eye out for major events that may affect your trade.

A perfect example of this hybrid strategy occurred during my trading of the EUR/USD pair. Fundamental study indicated a declining Eurozone economy compared to a robust US economy, implying future euro depreciation.

The daily chart displayed a descending triangle pattern, indicating a bearish formation. When the price fell below the triangle's support, coinciding with a weaker-than-expected Eurozone GDP report, I opened a short trade.

I controlled the trade utilising technical levels for stop-loss and take-profit orders, while keeping an eye out for forthcoming economic data. This strategy enabled me to ride a substantial slump, yielding one of my most profitable swing bets.

What is the key takeaway? Neither technical nor fundamental analysis provides the complete picture. The combination of these tactics can provide you an advantage in forex swing trading.

As we complete this chapter, keep in mind that these techniques, technical and fundamental analysis, are more than just theoretical concepts. They are practical tools that you will utilise on a daily basis throughout your trading career. Mastering any talent requires time and practice. But with practice, you'll become more competent at reading the forex market's complex language.

In our next chapter, we'll get into the specifics of developing your swing trading technique. We'll look at how to use the tools we've reviewed to create a tailored approach that fits your goals and risk tolerance. Are you ready to start developing your own trading edge? Let us move on!

CHAPTER 4

Crafting Your Swing Trading Strategy

Now that we've armed ourselves with the necessary tools for technical and fundamental research, it's time to combine these parts into a cohesive swing trading plan. Remember, there is no one-size-fits-all method to forex trading. Your plan should be as individual as your fingerprint, adapted to your objectives, risk tolerance, and lifestyle.

Entry and Exit Strategies that Work

The key to any effective swing trading technique is knowing when to enter and quit trades. Let's look at some effective approaches:

Trend-following entries: Riding the trend is a traditional swing trading approach. Look for pullbacks in established trends to identify suitable entry opportunity. For example, in an uptrend, wait for the price to retrace to a significant support level or a moving average before taking a long position. This strategy helped me catch a fantastic uptrend in the AUD/USD. The pair has been profiting for weeks, and I was waiting for a fall to the 20-day moving average. When the price rallied off this level, I went long, riding the trend for another 200 pips.

Breakout Entries: Breakouts from consolidation patterns might mark the beginning of new trends. Look for prices to break above or below resistance, particularly if volume increases. A notable EUR/JPY trade springs to mind. The two had been forming a symmetrical triangle for weeks. When price eventually broke above the top trendline with significant momentum, I went long. The subsequent rally earned me a tidy 300-pip profit.

Reverse Entries: While more difficult, reversal trades can be extremely rewarding if timed correctly. Look for symptoms of weariness in the present trend, such as a divergence in price and momentum. I recall a USD/CAD trade in which the price was in a strong rise but the RSI indicated negative divergence. When the price failed to reach a new high and instead established a double top, I went short. The reversal that occurred was fast and beneficial.

Exit plans are equally important:

1. Set Take-Profit Orders using major resistance/support levels, Fibonacci extensions, or a fixed risk-reward ratio. In my swing trades, I normally aim for a risk-reward ratio of at least 1:2.

2. Trailing Stops: Lock in profits while letting winners run. You might place your stop behind a moving average or at a set distance from the current price.

3. Timed Exits: Exiting after a defined time period can be effective, especially if the planned move does not occur inside your expected timeframe.

Set Stop-Loss and Take-Profit: Your Safety Net.

The proper placement of stop-loss and take-profit orders is critical for risk management and profit protection. **Here's how to tackle this**:

Place stops beyond important support/resistance levels and use the Average True Range (ATR) indicator to account for market volatility.

- Only risk 1-2% of your money on a single trade.

A unpleasant lesson taught me the value of precise stop placement. Early in my career, I used an overly tight stop-loss on a GBP/USD trade. A tiny market fluctuation triggered my stop before the pair moved in the expected direction. Since then, I've always given my trades room to breathe, placing stops beyond major market structures.

Profitable Placement:

- Use Fibonacci extension levels to determine profit goals.
- Consider setting additional take-profit orders to earn partial earnings along the road.
- Align profit targets with psychological levels, such as round numbers, where prices may face resistance.

Position Sizing: Balancing Risk and Rewards

Position sizing is the unsung hero of effective trading. It is not only important to consider how much you might potentially earn, but also how much you can afford to lose.

Here's how to tackle it:

Percentage-Based Sizing: Risk a set percentage of your account on each trade.

For swing trading, 1-2% is usually sufficient. This strategy ensures that your position size adjusts automatically based on your account balance.

Fixed Dollar Amount: Some traders prefer to risk a specific amount per trade. Although simpler, this system does not account for changes in account size.

Use Volatility-Based Sizing: Adjust position size based on market volatility. In more turbulent markets, you may cut your investment size to keep the same dollar risk.

I discovered the hard way that overleveraging may be disastrous. In my early days, I risked 10% of my account on a single EUR/USD trades since I was confident in my research. When the trade went against me, I suffered a substantial loss that set me back several months. Since then, I've strictly adhered to risking no more than 2% per trade, allowing me to weather losing streaks without significantly affecting my account.

Adapting To Market Conditions

Markets are not static, nor should your strategy be. Here's how to maintain flexibility:

1. In trending markets, prioritise trend-following methods above range-based approaches. In range markets, look for opportunity to buy at support and sell at resistance.

2. Volatility Adjustment: Widen your stops and objectives during periods of extreme volatility. You may tighten them during periods of low volatility.

3. Correlation Awareness: Be aware of relationships between currency pairs. Trading many correlated pairs in the same direction may unintentionally raise your risk.

I recall a day when I was battling with my typical trend-following strategy. The markets appeared turbulent and directionless.

It wasn't until I switched to a range-trading approach, buying at support and selling at resistance, that I saw consistent returns again. This event showed me the need of versatility when trading.

Putting it All Together

Your swing trading strategy should combine all of these features. Here's the basic framework:

1. Analyse prospective trades using your favourite technical and fundamental analysis.

2. Ensure entrance signals fit with your chosen strategy.

3. Set stop-loss and take-profit levels according to market structure and risk tolerance.

4. Calculate position size to avoid risking more than 1-2% of your money.

5. Continually monitor and adjust to changing market conditions.

6. Exit based on specified criteria or if analysis indicates the trading idea is no longer applicable.

Remember that the ideal plan is one that you can follow consistently. It should be consistent with your personality, risk tolerance, and lifestyle. Don't be hesitant to try out new strategies on a demo account before investing real money.

CHAPTER 5

Risk Management: Protecting Your Capital

In the exciting world of forex swing trading, risk management is the unsung hero that distinguishes professionals from beginners. It's not only about making money; it's about remaining in the game long enough to reap the benefits. This chapter will go over the important principles of risk management that every swing trader must understand.

The 1% Rule is a lifesaver for beginners.

The 1% rule is a fundamental risk management technique that could literally rescue your trading account. This is how it works.

- Avoid risking more than 1% of your account balance on any single trade.

- For a $10,000 account, set a maximum risk of $100 each trade.

This rule has multiple purposes:

1. It safeguards against catastrophic losses.

2. It enables you to sustain losing trades without emptying your funds.

3. Focus on high-probability trades.

I discovered the significance of this guideline the hard way. Early in my trading career, I bet 10% of my account on a "sure thing" EUR/USD trade. When the market turned against me, I lost a large portion of my capital in one fell swoop. It took months to recover from that loss, both financially and emotionally.

Since implementing the 1% rule, I've been able to trade with greater confidence and consistency. Even during losing streaks, my account balance remains reasonably consistent, allowing me to stay in the game and take advantage of profitable possibilities when they emerge.

Emotional Control: Understanding the Trader's Mindset

Emotions are frequently the trader's worst adversary. Fear and greed can cause rash decisions that jeopardize even the best-laid trading plans.

Here are some ways for maintaining emotional control.

Stick to Your Plan: Develop and stick to your trading strategy. Do not let your emotions cause you to depart from your strategy.

Use Stop-Losses: Set stop-losses before starting a trade. This eliminates the emotional decision about when to exit a lost trade.

Practice Mindfulness: Meditation can help you stay calm and focused during trading sessions.

Keep a trading journal: Regularly evaluate your trades to identify emotional patterns and places for improvement.

Avoid overtrading: Do not feel obligated to stay in the market all the time. Sometimes the finest trade isn't even a trade.

I recall a time when I was battling with excessive trading. Every minor price change appeared to be an opportunity, and I found myself trading multiple times without sufficient analysis. This resulted in a sequence of minor losses that accumulated swiftly.

Only when I began practicing mindfulness and keeping a comprehensive trade log was I able to restore control. I learnt to identify the emotional triggers that lead to overtrading and devised techniques to combat them.

Dealing with Losses: Converting Setbacks into Comebacks

Losses are an unavoidable aspect of trading. It is not about avoiding losses entirely, but about handling them successfully. Here's how to handle losses:

1. Accept losses as part of the game. Understand that even the best traders lose trades. It is not personal; it is strictly business.

2. Analyse, Don't Agonise: After a loss trade, objectively evaluate what went wrong. Was there a mistake in your plan, or just typical market volatility?

3. Ensure Proper Position Sizing: Even after a loss, follow your risk management standards. Don't expand your position size in order to "make back" losses.

4. Take Breaks: If you're experiencing a losing run, taking a break can help you regain perspective.

5. Learn and adapt: Use losses to improve your trading strategy.

Following a streak of losses in GBP/USD trading, I had one of my most major learning experiences. Initially, I fell into the trap of raising my position sizes in an attempt to recoup my losses rapidly. This resulted in even larger losses.

It was a difficult lesson, but it taught me the value of consistency in position sizing and emotional resilience. I stepped back, extensively analysed my loss trades, and discovered areas for improvement in my method. When I returned to trading, I was more disciplined and hence more profitable.

The risk-reward ratio is the key to long-term profitability.

Long-term success in swing trading requires an understanding and implementation of a favourable risk-reward ratio. Here's why.

• A positive risk-reward ratio allows for profitability even with a victory rate below 50%.

If you risk 1% every trade and have a risk-reward ratio of 1:2, winning 4 out of 10 trades is enough to be successful.

How to create a favourable risk-reward ratio:

1. Determine your stop-loss based on technical levels rather than personal risk tolerance.

2. Set a take-profit ratio of at least 1:2 to balance risk and reward.

3. Be patient. Do not adjust your take-profit closer in order to close the trade faster.

I recall a EUR/JPY trade in which I identified a possible reversal at a critical resistance level. I positioned my stop-loss above the resistance and my take-profit at a support level, resulting in a 1:3 risk-reward ratio. The trade took more than a week to complete, which tested my patience. But when it finally reached my take-profit, the wait was totally worth it.

Diversification of Forex Trading

While the forex market is fairly diversified, appropriate diversification can further lower your risk.

1. Diversify your currency trading: Avoid relying just on one currency pair. Trading several pairings can help you diversify your risk.

2. Consider Correlations: Avoid doubling your risk by being aware of pair correlations.

3. Vary your trading techniques to suit different market conditions.

4. Time Diversification: Use diverse holding periods to reconcile short-term volatility with long-term trends.

In my own trade, I usually focus on three or four currency pairs, each with a distinct base currency. This strategy has helped me manage various market conditions while minimizing the influence of any single economic event on my overall portfolio.

Continuous Risk Assessment.

There is no such thing as a "set it and forget it" approach to risk management. It involves continuous evaluation and adjustment:

1. Regularly review your risk parameters. As your account expands (or shrinks), modify your position sizes to match.

2. Stay informed about market conditions, including future economic developments that may affect volatility.

3. Regularly review your risk tolerance: Your risk tolerance may change as you get more experience. Adjust your tactics accordingly.

4. Use technology wisely. Take advantage of your trading platform's risk management capabilities, but do not rely only on them.

Remember that good risk management is taking measured risks that are consistent with your trading objectives and risk tolerance. Implementing these tactics will prepare you to navigate the fascinating yet challenging world of FX swing trading.

In our next chapter, we'll look at how to create a comprehensive trading strategy that includes all of the factors we've covered so far. Are you prepared to put all of the pieces together and develop your road map to forex trading success? Let us move on!

CHAPTER 6

Put It All Together: Your Trading Plan

A well-crafted trading strategy is the foundation of profitable forex swing trading. It's your personal road map for making decisions and staying disciplined in the face of market turbulence. In this chapter, we will look at how to develop a thorough trading strategy that integrates everything that we've learnt thus far.

Setting realistic goals and expectations

Setting specific, attainable targets is the first stage in creating a trading plan. Remember that overnight success in forex trading is a fallacy.

Here's how to set goals:

1. Short-term goals: Prioritise procedure over profits.

2. Set medium-term goals, such as achieving a target monthly return or minimising maximum drawdown.

3. Set long-term goals: Consider where you want to go in a year or beyond. Perhaps you want to shift to full-time trading or reach a certain account size.

I learnt the value of setting realistic goals early in my career. Initially, I set an aggressive goal of doubling my account within three months. This false expectation resulted in overtrading and excessive risk-taking. My trading improved dramatically after I shifted my focus to steady execution and gradual growth.

Creating a Personalized Trading Schedule

Your trading timetable should be consistent with your lifestyle and the currency market's rhythm. Consider the following factors:

1. Identify the most convenient forex sessions (Asian, European, or North American) for your schedule.

2. Currency Pairs: Select the most active pairs for your trading hours.

3. Set a daily time commitment for trading. Swing trading usually takes less time than day trading, but more than position trading.

4. Schedule time for pre-market analysis and post-trade assessment.

My own schedule has developed over time. Initially, I attempted to trade during the overlap between the European and North American sessions, believing it would provide the best possibilities. However, this conflicted with my regular employment. I eventually settled on analysing charts and setting up trades in the nights, focussing on pairs like AUD/USD and NZD/USD, which frequently move throughout the Asian session.

Define Your Trading Strategy.

Your strategy is the foundation of your trading plan. It should explicitly outline

1. Trade Selection Criteria: What conditions must be met before considering a trade?

2. Entry Rules: Specific triggers for starting a trade. Consider the following scenario: "Enter long when price breaks above the 50-day moving average and RSI is above 50."

3. Exit Rules: For both profit and loss. Be as precise as possible.

4. Position Sizing: How will you calculate the amount of each trade?

5. Risk management: Set maximum risk per trade and overall account limitations.

My swing trading method involves identifying pullbacks in established trends on a daily chart. A bullish engulfing candle at a support level, verified by an RSI reading above 40, serves as an entry trigger. The initial stop loss is set below the trough of the engulfing candle. Take-profit is set at the nearest resistance level to provide at least a 1:2 risk-reward ratio. The position size is set to risk 1% of my account on each trade."

Back-testing and Forward Testing: Your Strategy

Before committing actual wealth, it is critical to test your strategy:

1. Backtesting: Test your strategy against past data. This can be done manually or with trading software.

2. Forward Testing (Paper Trading) allows you to test your strategy in real-time market conditions without risking real money.

When backtesting, consider the following: win rate, average win/loss, maximum drawdown, and profit factor (gross profit divided by gross loss).

I spent several weeks backtesting my pullback technique on daily EUR/USD and GBP/USD charts over a two-year timeframe. The data revealed a 58% win rate with a 1:1.8 average risk-reward ratio, giving me the confidence to switch to paper trading.

During forward testing, I realised that my initial stop-loss placement was frequently excessively tight, being triggered by normal market noise. The performance of my plan improved dramatically once I adjusted this feature.

Adapting Your Plan As You Grow

Your trading strategy should be a live document that adapts as you gain expertise and market conditions change. Regular review and adjustment are critical.

1. Conduct monthly performance reviews to analyse trading performances. Look for patterns in your successful and losing trades.

2. Evaluate market conditions: Are there variations in volatility or trending behaviour among your chosen pairs?

3. Refine your plan by making tiny, incremental modifications based on reviews. Avoid frequent and abrupt changes.

4. Personal Development: Identify areas for improvement in your abilities and expertise.

I examine my trading plan quarterly. During one analysis, I saw that my win percentage on short trades was significantly lower than on long trades. This caused me to change my criteria for short entries, which improved my total result.

Key elements of a comprehensive trading plan

To summarize, your trading plan should contain:

1. Personal Trading Goals.

2. Risk Management Rules.

3. Detailed Trading Strategy.

4. Trading Schedule.

5. Recommended Trading Pairs and Timeframes

6. Position Sizing Method

7. Process for keeping and reviewing records

8. Continuous Education Plan

Remember, a strong trading plan should include:

- Clear and unambiguous
- Realistic and achievable
- Adaptable to changing market conditions
- Aligned with personal goals and risk tolerance.

A Personal Perspective on the Importance of a Trading Plan

In my early days of trading, I lacked a solid strategy. Each trade was made independently, frequently based on gut instinct or the most recent "hot tip." The end effect was erratic performance and emotional stress.

Creating a solid trading plan was a watershed moment in my forex journey. It gave my trading a structure, eliminated most of the emotional decision-making, and enabled me to analyse and improve my performance in a systematic manner.

One particularly remarkable moment occurred during the Brexit referendum in 2016. The markets were extremely turbulent, with many traders making rash moves. My trading strategy has already dictated how I would handle such high-impact situations. I followed my guidelines, avoided overtrading, and made a profit during that difficult era while many others failed.

In the currency market, your trading plan serves as a compass. It keeps you on track when market circumstances are hazy, directs your actions when opportunities come, and helps you stay disciplined when emotions try to take over.

CHAPTER 7

Real-Life Swing Trading Case Studies

Theory is important, but nothing beats the insights learnt from actual trading experiences. In this chapter, we'll look at three case studies that demonstrate the principles we've discussed thus far. These examples will show you how to execute your swing trading strategy, manage risk, and adjust to changing market conditions.

Case Study 1: Riding the Trend in EUR/USD.

Setup: In late 2022, the EUR/USD pair was in a strong rise on the daily charts. For several weeks, the pair had been making higher highs and higher lows, with dynamic support provided by the 20-day Exponential Moving Average (EMA).

Analysis:

• Daily and 4-hour charts show a clear bullish trend. • Support comes from the 20-day EMA and prior swing low. • Resistance comes from the recent swing high. • RSI indicates bullish momentum but not overbought.

Following a brief decline to the 20-day EMA, a bullish engulfing candle appeared. This met our entry criterion for a trend continuation trade.

Trade management:

• Entry point: 1.0520 • Stop loss: 1.0480, below the low of the engulfing candle (40 pips risk).

• Take profit at the last swing high of 1.0620 (target 100 pips).

• Risk-reward ratio is 1:2.5.

The trade proceeded as expected, reaching the take profit level within a week. This scenario highlights the value of trading with the trend and use key technical levels for entry and exit.

Key Takeaway: Patience in waiting for the right setup in a strong trend can result in high probability trades with favourable risk-reward ratios.

Case Study 2: How to Navigate a Range-Bound Market in GBP/JPY

Setup: For several weeks in mid-2023, GBP/JPY traded in a distinct range, bouncing between support at 160.00 and resistance at 162.50.

Analysis:

• Market Structure: Clearly defined trading range.

• Support: Multiple touches around 160.00 • Resistance: Several rejections at 162.50 • RSI oscillates between overbought and oversold levels.

Entry: As the price reached the support level, a bullish hammer candle appeared on the 4-hour chart. The RSI was also oversold, indicating a possible bounce.

Trade management:

• Entry number: 160.20.

• Set a stop loss below the hammer low at 159.80 (40 pips risk).

• Take profit in the mid-range at 161.25 (105 pips goal).

• Risk-reward ratio is 1:2.6.

After three days, the trade had achieved its take profit level. This example shows how to efficiently trade in a range-bound market by buying near support and selling near resistance.

Key takeaway: Not all markets are trending. Recognizing and adjusting to range-bound conditions can result in recurring trading opportunities.

Case Study 3: Managing a Losing Trade in AUD/USD.

Setup: In early 2024, the daily chart of AUD/USD displayed indicators of a potential trend reversal. Following an extended downtrend, the pair developed a double bottom pattern and broke above a falling trend-line.

Analysis:

• Market Structure: Possible trend reversal.

• Support at double bottom level

• Resistance at previous swing high

• MACD indicates bullish crossover.

A breakout above the neckline of the double bottom prompted our entrance.

Trade management:

• Entry: 0.6580

• Stop Loss: Below breakout level at 0.6540 (40 pips risk)

- Take profit at the last swing high of 0.6680 (target 100 pips).

- Risk-reward ratio is 1:2.5.

However, the breakout failed, and the price rapidly reverted. Our stop loss was hit, causing a 40-pip loss.

Post-Trade Analysis: Although the setup appeared promising, the overall market sentiment turned due to unexpected economic data. This emphasizes the significance of being current on fundamental aspects that may affect your trading.

Key Takeaway: Not every trade will be profitable. Proper risk management ensures that losses remain minimal and controllable.

Lessons from Case Studies

1. The EUR/USD example demonstrates how trading in the direction of a trend can result in high-probability setups.

2. Adapt to Market Conditions: The GBP/JPY example highlights the significance of understanding and adjusting to diverse market structures.

3. Proper risk management is crucial, as demonstrated by the AUD/USD scenario. Proper stop loss placement can lessen the impact of losing trades.

4. Patience Pays Off: Waiting for clear setups that correspond with our technique resulted in improved trading performance.

5. Continuous Learning: Every trade, win or lose, teaches essential lessons for progress.

Personal Reflection.

These case studies remind me of my own trading experiences. I recall a comparable EUR/USD trade early in my career that I prematurely stopped due to impatience, costing me considerable winnings. This taught me the value of letting successful trades run.

The range-bound GBP/JPY scenario reflects a period in which I struggled to adapt my trend-following method to sideways markets. Learning to recognize and trade ranges greatly enhanced my total performance.

Finally, the AUD/USD loss reflects a large number of trades in which unexpected news took me off guard. It underlined the importance of always being aware of potential fundamental catalysts that could affect my technical setups.

Real-world trading is rarely as simple as textbook examples might suggest. Studying these case studies and reflecting on your own trades will help you gain the experience and intuition needed to successfully navigate the complex forex markets.

Remember that every trade is a learning opportunity. Always analyze your decisions and results, whether you win or lose. This constant improvement process distinguishes successful traders from the rest.

In our next chapter, we'll look at advanced tactics for honing your swing trading talents. Are you prepared to take your trading to the next level? Let us press on!

CHAPTER 8

Evolving as a Forex Swing Trader

As you go through your forex swing trading adventure, continuous growth becomes increasingly important. This chapter focusses on tactics for honing your trading talents, staying ahead of market trends, and establishing a successful trading career.

Continuous Learning and Improvement.

1. Maintain Market Knowledge: The forex market is always changing due to global economic and political developments. Staying informed is critical:

- Follow credible financial news sources.
- Regularly review economic calendars.

- Understand how different events affect currency pairs.

Personal Experience: Early in my career, I underestimated the importance of central bank meetings. A sudden rate decision once caught me off guard, causing a large loss. Since then, I've made it a practice to regularly follow economic calendars and central bank communications.

2. Develop your technical analysis skills. While simple chart patterns and indicators are useful, advanced techniques can provide further insights:

- Learn Elliott Wave Theory for trend analysis, as well as Fibonacci retracements and extensions.
- Conduct intermarket analysis to identify linkages among markets.

Tip: Do not attempt to master everything at once. Gradually include new strategies into your analysis, verifying their usefulness before fully implementing them.

3. Improve Your Fundamental Analysis: Understanding why price changes occur will help you make better trading decisions.

Investigate how economic indicators influence currency values.

Learn to understand central bank statements and analyse long-term economic trends across countries.

Personal Insight: Combining fundamental analysis with my technical technique has greatly enhanced my ability to anticipate and ride long-term trends.

4. Developing your thinking is equally crucial as mastering the markets.

- Mindfulness can increase focus and emotional control.

- Routines can help maintain discipline.
- Review and reflect on trading performance often.

Exercise: Keep a trading notebook that records not just your trades but also your emotions and cognitive processes. This can aid in identifying psychological trends that influence your trading.

Staying ahead of market trends.

Embrace Technology: As technology advances, so does the trading scene.

- Explore algorithmic trading concepts.
- Utilize modern charting software to improve analysis.
- Consider using trade journals and analytics tools to monitor performance.

Caution: While technology can help you trade more effectively, it cannot replace smart strategy and risk management.

2. Adapt to Changing Market Conditions: Markets undergo many phases, including trending, range, turbulent, and tranquil.

- Create tactics tailored to diverse market conditions.
- Recognize market shifts and adjust your approach accordingly.

Example: Market volatility skyrocketed during the COVID-19 epidemic. Traders who swiftly adjusted their methods to accommodate larger price fluctuations were better positioned to seize opportunities.

3. Connect with other traders to gain vital insights and assistance.

- Join online trading groups or local meetups.

- To improve your trading skills, consider attending webinars and seminars, seeking mentorship, or joining a trading group.

Personal Story: Joining a forex trading group exposed me to a variety of opinions and tactics. This not only broadened my understanding but also offered moral support during difficult trading moments.

Developing a Sustainable Trading Career

Risk Management Evolution: As your account expands, you may need to change your risk management approach.

- Review and alter position sizing on a regular basis. - Scale into larger trades.
- Implement portfolio risk management.

Rule of thumb: Never risk more than 1-2% of your account on a single trade, regardless of its size.

Diversification Strategies: Specialization has advantages, yet diversification can improve stability.

- Trade various currency pairs.
- Consider adding other financial instruments, such as CFDs on indices or commodities.
- Explore several timeframes for swing trading.

Caution: Only diversify into areas you fully understand. Expanding too hastily into unknown markets can result in avoidable losses.

Develop a Business Mindset: Approach trading as a business to achieve long-term success.

- Develop a detailed business plan for trading.
- Maintain meticulous records for performance tracking and tax purposes.
- Determine the legal structure of your trading activity (e.g., sole proprietorship or LLC).

Tip: Speak with a financial counsellor or accountant about the tax implications of your trading activities.

4. **Maintaining a work-life balance** :is essential for long-term success in trading.

To avoid burnout, establish clear boundaries between trading and personal time, maintain outside hobbies and relationships, and take regular pauses.

Personal Insight: I previously became extremely obsessed with trading, which resulted in stress and poor results. Establishing a disciplined regimen with allocated non-trading time had a huge impact on both my personal life and trading performance.

Continuous approach Refinement: Your trading approach should evolve with experience.

- Regularly back-test and forward test your methods.
- Implement tiny, incremental modifications instead of major overhauls.

- Be willing to delete outdated elements.

Exercise: Conduct a quarterly evaluation of your trading approach. Do an analysis to determine what is working well and what could use some improvement.

Evolving as a forex swing trader is a constant process. It needs a dedication to lifelong learning, adaptability to changing market conditions, and a comprehensive approach to personal and professional development. Remember, the goal is not only to improve your trading skills, but also to establish a long-term and rewarding trading profession.

When using these methods, remember to stick to your primary trading ideas and risk management standards. In foreign exchange trading, achieving success is more of a marathon than a sprint.

With patience, dedication, and a growth attitude, you can overcome the obstacles and realize the benefits of FX swing trading.

In our final chapter, we'll summarize the important points from this book and offer advice on your future steps as a developing FX swing trader. Are you ready to begin this lifelong path of growth and improvement? Let's wrap up our discussion about forex swing trading!

CONCLUSION

Your Journey Begins

As we approach the last chapter of "Forex Swing Trading For Beginners: Mastering the Art of Swing Trading in Forex," it's time to review the major takeaways and prepare you for the exciting trip ahead. Remember, this book is not the end, but rather the beginning of your journey into the world of FX swing trading.

Recap: Key Swing Trading Principles

1. Understanding the Forex Markets:

The FX market is the world's largest financial market, functioning continuously around the clock.

Currency pairs are the main trading instruments, with major, minor, and exotic pairs providing various options.

2. The Basics of Swing Trading:

Swing trading tries to capture medium-term price fluctuations by holding positions for days or weeks.

It strikes a compromise between the high-stress environment of day trading and the lengthy wait times of position trading.

3. Technical analysis.

Swing trading analysis focusses on price action, chart patterns, and technical indicators.

Key tools include trend lines, support and resistance levels, moving averages, and momentum indicators such as RSI and MACD.

4. Fundamental analysis:

Economic factors, central bank policies, and geopolitical events have a considerable impact on currency movements.

Combining fundamental and technical analysis offers a more thorough trading technique.

5. Risk management:

The 1% rule states that traders should never risk more than 1% of their capital on a single trade.

Use stop-loss orders regularly to safeguard your capital.

Aim for a positive risk-reward ratio, ideally 1:2 or above.

6. Emotional control.

Create a trading plan and stick to it to avoid making emotional decisions.

- Be patient - not every market change presents a trading opportunity.
- Learn from losses, but don't be discouraged.

7. Continuous learning:

- Stay up-to-date on forex market news and trends.
- Regularly analyse and adjust your trading approach.
- Connect with other traders and find a mentor.

Encouragement and Final Thoughts

Starting your forex swing trading experience is both exhilarating and demanding. To wrap things up, consider the following:

1. Start small: Use a demo account to test your technique without risking real money. When you begin live trading, start with small position sizes. Remember that safeguarding your capital is critical to long-term success.

2. Embrace the Learning Curve: Successful traders were once beginners. Don't be discouraged by early losses; instead, think of them as tuition for real-world trading education. Analyze each trade, learn from your mistakes, and keep improving.

3. Develop Your Edge: With expertise, you'll identify the optimal market conditions for your plan. This is your trading advantage. Refine it, focus on it, and be prepared to wait for these high-probability circumstances.

4. Be Committed, But Flexible: Consistency is essential in trading. Stick to your trading strategy, but be prepared to adjust if market conditions alter.

The most successful traders are those who can adapt to changing market conditions.

5. Balance Risk and Reward: Forex trading offers high potential for profit, but also comes with substantial hazards. Always prioritize risk management. It is not about how much money you can make; rather, it is about how much money you can keep.

6. Develop Patience: Swing trading demands patience. You won't (or shouldn't) be in the market all the time. Learning to wait for the ideal settings is an important skill that will benefit you much.

Personal Reflection.

Allow me to give a personal anecdote that captures the forex swing trading experience. When I first started, I was eager to trade every day, believing that more trades equaled more profits. This resulted in overtrading and avoidable losses.

It wasn't until I learnt to be patient and wait for high-probability setups that fitted with my technique that I started making consistent profits. A single EUR/USD trade stood out.

After several days of no trading, I observed a beautiful setup: a pullback to a crucial support level in an uptrend, accompanied by bullish candlestick patterns and RSI divergence.

I initiated the trade with good risk management, establishing stop-loss and take-profit levels that corresponded to my risk-reward ratio of 1:2. The trade took a week to complete, which tested my patience. But when it reached my take-profit point, I not only made a substantial profit, but I also learnt the importance of quality over quantity in trading.

This experience taught me that success in forex swing trading requires accurate, well-timed actions based on a good plan and unyielding dedication.

Resources for Further Learning

Your educational path does not end with this book. Here are some websites to help you continue your Forex education:

1. Online education: Udemy and Coursera provide comprehensive forex trading education.

2. Economic Calendars: Websites like ForexFactory offer extensive calendars for fundamental research.

3. Join forex forums and social media groups to communicate with other traders.

4. Most brokers provide demo accounts. Use these to practise without incurring financial risk.

Remember, forex swing trading is not a get-rich-quick scheme, but rather a talent that takes time, effort, and ongoing study to perfect. Be patient with yourself, stay focused on your study, and always prioritize risk management.

As you finish this book and open your charts, remember that every master trader began exactly where you are today. Your quest to mastering forex swing trading starts today. Accept the challenges, cherish your achievements, and never stop learning. The FX market awaits you; are you ready to make your mark?

I hope this message finds you well and that you enjoyed reading my book, Forex Swing Trading for Beginners

Your support and feedback mean the world to me.

If you have a moment, I would be incredibly grateful if you could leave a review on Amazon. Your honest thoughts and feedback not only help me improve but also assist other readers in discovering the book.

Thank you so much for your time and support!

Warm regards,

James Willy

Access Your Exclusive Video Series!

Thank you for purchasing the book! To improve your learning experience, below is an exclusive video series just for you. This series goes deeper into some of the principles discussed in the book, including step-by-step video tutorials to help you understand the material.

Access the Video Series Here:

https://mega.nz/folder/IYZRQZTL#UIoA3WK6Gb_OfS2Xxq-iRA

Simply click the link above to access the videos and improve your trading abilities. Happy learning and trading!

www.ingramcontent.com/pod-product-compliance
Lightning Source LLC
Chambersburg PA
CBHW050325230526
45471CB00005B/2353